MW01490280

Native American Chiefs
and Warriors

Seminole Chief
Osceola

William R. Sanford

Enslow Publishers, Inc.
40 Industrial Road
Box 398
Berkeley Heights, NJ 07922
USA

http://www.enslow.com

Original edition published as *Osceola: Seminole Warrior* in 1994.

Library of Congress Cataloging-in-Publication Data

Sanford, William R. (William Reynolds), 1927-
Seminole chief Osceola / William R. Sanford.
    p. cm. — (Native American chiefs and warriors)
Includes bibliographical references and index.
ISBN 978-0-7660-4117-2
1. Osceola, Seminole chief, 1804–1838—Juvenile literature. 2. Seminole Indians—Kings and rulers—Biography—Juvenile literature. I. Title.
E99.S28O848 2013
975.9004'973859092—dc23
[B]
                                         2011050996

Future editions:
Paperback ISBN 978-1-4644-0263-0
ePUB ISBN 978-1-4645-1168-4
PDF ISBN 978-1-4646-1168-1

Printed in China
062012 Leo Paper Group, Heshan City, Guangdong, China
10 9 8 7 6 5 4 3 2 1

To Our Readers: We have done our best to make sure all Internet addresses in this book were active and appropriate when we went to press. However, the author and the publisher have no control over and assume no liability for the material available on those Internet sites or on other Web sites they may link to. Any comments or suggestions can be sent by e-mail to comments@enslow .com or to the address on the back cover.

Photo Credits: *A History of Florida* by Caroline Mays Brevard, American Book Company, pp. 23, 36; ©Clipart.com, pp. 6, 16, 31; ©Enslow Publishers, Inc., p. 21; Florida State Archives, p. 19; Library of Congress, pp. 11, 17, 24, 27, 35, 39, 40.

Cover Photo: Paul Daly

Contents

Author's Note

This book tells the true story of the Seminole warrior Osceola. Many mistakenly think he was the chief of all his tribe. But his true fame rests on his leadership in war. He led the Seminoles' fight against the U.S. Army. At the time the press rushed to print stories about Osceola. Some were made up, but others were true. The events described in this book all really happened.

Osceola has not been forgotten. Three counties, two mountains, and a national forest carry his name.[1] There are also twenty towns named Osceola.

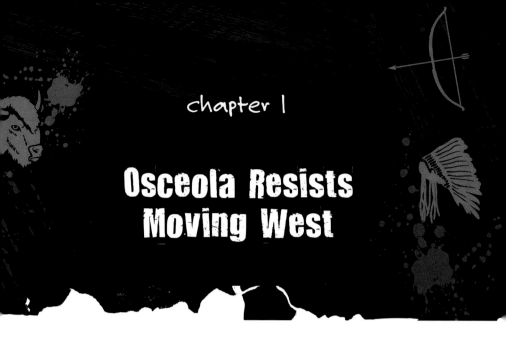

chapter 1

Osceola Resists Moving West

Wiley Thompson glared at Osceola. Would the young Seminole block his well-laid plan? Thompson was the Indian agent at Fort King, Florida. His job was to carry out U.S. government policy on the Seminole reservation.

Now, in 1835, Thompson had summoned the Seminole chiefs for a talk. The government wanted the Seminoles' land. He told the chiefs they would have to move. They each made their mark on a treaty. Thompson gave the bands of these chiefs a nine-month delay. During this time the bands could harvest crops and round up cattle. They would arrive in the West in time for spring planting. Five chiefs did not sign. In anger Thompson slashed their names from the list of chiefs.

Thompson then looked to Osceola. The Seminole stood with his arms folded across his chest. At thirty-one he stood five feet, eight inches. His walk was firm. And he had a handsome open look. His eyes were calm; his nose, straight; and his lips, thin.[1]

Osceola moved forward. He returned Thompson's glare. Drawing his knife, he stabbed it into the wood of the table. "This is the only way I sign," he cried[2] Then Osceola yanked out his blade. And with the stride of a hunter, he left the fort.

Thompson feared the Seminoles might fight rather than move. So he issued an order. The fort would sell the tribe no more lead, powder, or guns. Osceola was angry. A few days later he stamped into Thompson's office.

Osceola stabbed the treaty that paid the Seminoles. They had taken money in return for agreeing to move out of Florida.

Osceola warned, "I will make the white man red with blood. . . . Then [I will] blacken him in the sun and rain. The wolf shall smell of his bones. The buzzard [shall] live upon his flesh."[3]

In June, Osceola came again to Fort King. With him was his wife Morning Dew, who was part black. A slave trader claimed that she was a runaway slave. He would take her away with him. Thompson listened to the argument. He said there was no proof the woman was not a runaway. The trader clapped her in irons and took her away. Osceola strongly objected. Thompson ordered soldiers to put Osceola in the fort prison. They put shackles on his ankles. He sat silently for two days.

In speaking to Osceola, Thompson revealed what lay behind his actions. Would the Seminole agree to persuade all the chiefs to move? If so he could go free. At the end of six days Osceola agreed to do what Thompson wanted. Once he was free he left the fort. When he reached the edge of the woods Osceola turned. He roared, "Yo he e hee!"[4] It was the Seminole war cry.

The Seminole chiefs met. All agreed to resist Thompson's plan. They would kill any chief who agreed to move. Charley Emathla was among the chiefs who refused to move. But in November he changed his mind. Charley had agreed to take his band to Fort Brooke. There, ships were waiting to take his band west.

1

At Fort King, Emathla sold his band's cattle. He received a small bag of coins in payment. On his way home Emathla was surrounded by twelve warriors led by Osceola. Osceola asked Emathla to join in the fight against the whites. When Emathla refused, Osceola fired his gun twice. Emathla fell to the ground dead. Osceola then picked up the bag of coins. "This is made of red men's blood," he cried.[5] He threw the coins into the woods. With this murder, Osceola began the Second Seminole War.

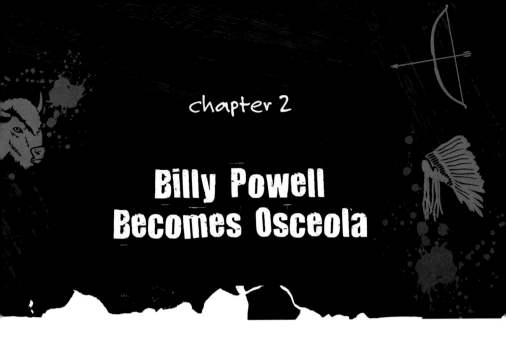

chapter 2

Billy Powell Becomes Osceola

O sceola was born in 1804 in what is now Macon County, Alabama. His name at birth was Billy Powell. His mother, "Polly" was half Creek, half Scot. She told Billy his father was a Creek warrior. He had died before Billy was born. Around that time Polly married William Powell. Powell, a lean quiet Englishman, was a trader. He traded with the Creeks for skins and blankets.

The family lived in a square one-room cabin. Pine logs formed the walls, and pine bark thatched the steep roof. A few blankets separated, the living quarters from Powell's trade goods that filled one end of the cabin. Billy slept on a wooden bench covered with deer skins. Near the house grew a few rows of vegetables, corn, and melons.

In 1812, the United States and England went to war. The Creeks divided their loyalty between the two countries. One branch, the White Sticks, sided with the Americans.

The other, the Red Sticks, aided the British. The Red Sticks killed three hundred settlers and soldiers at Fort Mims, Alabama. Two years later Andrew Jackson defeated the Red Sticks at the Battle of Horseshoe Bend. Troops from Georgia surged through the region. They killed every Creek they found. The soldiers did not care which branch of the tribe a Creek belonged to.

One day Powell went into the woods with his musket. He never returned. Polly knew the white soldiers must be coming close. She crammed what little she owned into two packs. Then she and Billy joined a band of Red Sticks fleeing south. They all hoped to find safety in Florida, which was Spanish land then.

But mother and son could not keep up with the band. So they finished the five-hundred-mile trip alone. At last they reached the sand hills of west Florida. There they lived in the village of Peter McQueen, Polly's uncle. The village lay on high ground above a river. The river was full of fish, and the soil was fertile.

In 1815, McQueen's band moved near the Spanish town of St. Marks. There they mingled with the Seminoles. The Seminoles were a branch of the Creeks. They once lived in the southeastern United States. By the mid-1700s, the Creek homeland was overcrowded. So the Seminoles moved south to Florida.

Troubles on the Florida border led to the First Seminole War. In 1818, Jackson invaded Florida. He attacked McQueen's

This drawing of Osceola accurately portrays the Seminole leader's dress and weapons.

village, killing thirty-seven braves. Jackson captured Billy and his mother. When he released them, they went to a village on Tampa Bay. There Billy grew to manhood.

Each June the band staged a Green Corn Dance. At that time young men such as Billy went through a ceremony to become a warrior. Billy dressed in a blue breech clout. He wore leggings and soft moccasins. Quills and plumes trimmed his headband. Red paint covered his chest. Billy's earlobes were slit and then lengthened with weights. A medicine man scratched him with a needle. Soon Billy bled from the arms, legs, chest, and back. Bleeding, the Seminoles believed, purified the blood. The medicine man handed Billy a bowl of Asi, the Black Drink. It contained ground snakeroot, willow bark, red bay, wild grapes, and roots.[1]

While the medicine man sang, Billy drank the drink. At once he was ill, retching until it seemed he would die. When he stopped, the medicine man gave Billy a new name, Asi Yahola. The name meant Black Drink Singer. Years later, an Indian agent wrote down the name the way he heard it. So Asi Yahola became Osceola.

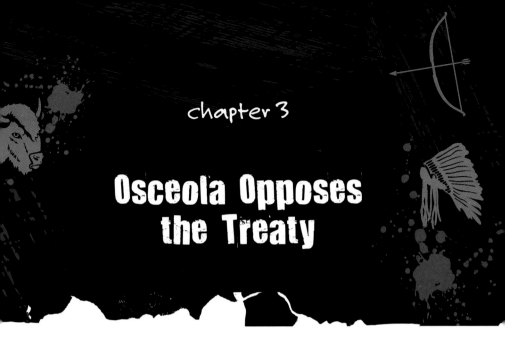

chapter 3

Osceola Opposes the Treaty

I n 1819, Osceola was a teenager. In that year Spain signed the Adams-Onis Treaty. The treaty gave Florida to the United States. The U.S. government thought the treaty gave it title to all Seminole lands. A Supreme Court case stated: "What is the Indian title? It is mere occupancy for the purpose of hunting. It is not like our tenures. They have no idea of a title to the soil itself. . . . It is not a true and legal possession."[1]

The treaty stated that all people in Florida were U.S. citizens. It did not exclude Seminoles or blacks. Yet no one enforced this part of the treaty. For decades runaway slaves had fled to Florida. The Seminoles treated them well. The slaves lived in their own villages, tending cattle and growing crops. Now the whites wanted to move the Seminoles to the West. Then they could take the Seminole lands. And slave traders would reenslave all blacks.

In 1821, Andrew Jackson was governor of Florida. He knew it would be hard to round up the Seminoles. The four thousand Seminoles were scattered across the state. North Florida was a wilderness, with rivers and lakes dotting the region. Oak, cedar, and sweet bay trees made dense forests. Myrtle and moss hung from the trees. And palmetto thickets filled the scrub lands.

In south Florida the Everglades covered the land. Miles of watery grasses carpeted these vast swamps. It would be hard to force the Seminoles out of these wilderness areas. It made more sense to limit their lands. In 1823, the U.S. government sent James Gadsden to make a treaty with the Seminoles.

The two parties met a few miles south of St. Augustine at Moultrie Creek. It is likely that Osceola came to the meeting. But the nineteen-year-old played no part. He was not yet a chief or war leader. He was a member of a band led by Chief Micanopy. He was top chief of the Seminoles.

The Seminoles agreed to sign a treaty. It set aside a big tract of land in central and south Florida. Whites would be free to cross the land. And the Seminoles promised not to roam from it to the coasts. They also promised not to help runaway slaves. The U.S. government promised to give the Seminoles $5,000 a year for twenty years. This money would pay for their moving costs and allow them to buy livestock. The U.S. government would also provide a school, blacksmith, and gunsmith. The total came to $221,000. In return, the Seminoles gave up twenty-eight million acres of land.

About this time Osceola moved to central Florida. He settled near Fort King. Osceola built a home on high ground. The hilly region lay amid an oak forest. Here Osceola became a leader. He had two wives, cattle, and a horse. In his fields, he tried to grow corn. But the Seminoles found it hard to raise crops on their new land, because the soil was poor. Some returned north. Others raided the settlers' farms for food.

In south Florida the Everglades covered the land. Miles of watery grasses carpeted these vast swamps.

In 1829, Jackson became president. He wanted to move the Seminoles out of Florida. He claimed that they would be better off in Oklahoma. In 1832, the U.S. government proposed a new treaty. They sent Gadsden to deal with the Seminoles. A group of chiefs met with Gadsden, and Osceola was among them.

The new treaty provided that seven chiefs would go to inspect the western lands. If they were satisfied, the Seminoles were to leave Florida within three years.

The Seminoles used dugout canoes to skim across the shallow waters of Florida swamplands.

A Seminole camp in Florida around 1835.

One third would go west each year. The Seminoles would receive $80,000 for their Florida land. That came to around two cents an acre! Fifteen chiefs and subchiefs made their marks.

Later the Seminoles said the treaty was a fraud. They claimed the interpreters had not really explained the treaty to them. Some thought they had agreed only to the inspection trip. Micanopy said he had never made his mark at all. The treaty outraged Osceola and many other Seminoles.

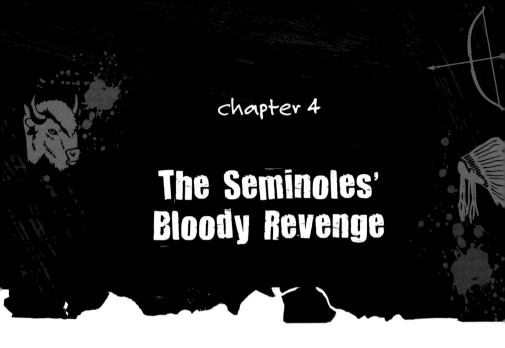

chapter 4

The Seminoles' Bloody Revenge

The Seminoles knew the killing of Charley Emathla would lead to war. They chose Osceola to lead them in battle. He ordered his people to leave the Fort King area. They would gather in the swamps farther south. A road ran from Fort King to Fort Brooke. Osceola ordered the burning of all bridges on that road.

King Philip led the eastern Seminoles. Osceola sent word: In twenty-five days the sixty-year-old chief should attack. On schedule Philip's men raided farms and mills. Within two weeks, they destroyed the entire sugar industry.

Osceola trained his men. He taught them to fight from behind trees. And if he gave the order, they would run away. In battle they must try to stay alive. Then they could strike the white people again. In December 1835, Osceola led eighty Seminoles on a raid. They attacked a wagon train.

Osceola was the chief of all the Seminoles. He only took action after conferring with other Seminole leaders.

His men drove off thirty mounted troops, killing six. This raid at Black Point opened the Second Seminole War.

General Duncan Clinch headed the U.S. forces in Florida. He had only 536 troops and 150 volunteers. These few men could not hunt down the scattered Seminoles. President Andrew Jackson blamed Clinch himself for the lack of success. But Jackson forgot that he won the First Seminole War with 35,000 troops, not 700.

On December 23, Major Francis Dade and 108 men left Fort Brooke. They would march one hundred miles north to Fort King. Osceola sent his next in command Jumper and his men to attack the slow-moving troops. He planned to join Jumper's force when he was finished with his job at Fort King.

Then Osceola led sixty men to the fort. For two days they waited in the brush. About 3 P.M. on December 28, General

Wiley Thompson left the fort. He walked toward a nearby trading post. He hoped to enjoy a cigar on his after-dinner stroll. The Seminoles opened fire. Fourteen bullets hit Thompson, and he fell dead at once. The warriors scalped his body, each brave taking a small piece. Osceola then led them to the trading post. They killed the three whites working there. After looting the store, they set it afire. Then they blended into the forest. Osceola had his revenge for his imprisonment.

Meanwhile Dade's column moved north through the swamps. A thousand-pound cannon slowed its progress. The bridges the column came to lay in smoking ruins. The troops crossed some streams on fallen logs. Ahead lay the Big Wahoo swamp. There the Seminoles lay waiting.

On the night of December 27, the Seminoles held a council. Jumper said they could wait no longer. The troops were nearing Fort King. All the chiefs gave their consent. A war dance began at once, lasting two hours.

Early the next morning the troops began their march. Soon the road entered a pine forest. Major Dade rode at the front of his men. From hiding, a warrior took aim. His first shot hit Dade, who fell dead from the saddle. At once the other Seminoles opened fire. Their first volley killed fifty soldiers.

The soldiers opened fire with the cannon. Jumper ordered his men to pull back. He had lost only three men, while two-thirds of the white troops were dead. The surviving soldiers cut down trees. They built a low three-sided fort. There they brought the wounded. Soon the cannon became useless, because there were no more cannonballs. Jumper ordered a charge. One by one the soldiers dropped. The warriors then entered the fort. They picked up the soldiers' weapons. Behind them came fifty runaway slaves. They slit the throats of the wounded, leaving no soldiers alive.

That night Osceola and his men met with Jumper's force. The Seminoles drank, sang, and danced all night. They had won more than a battle. They proved they might defeat the plan to move them west.

Osceola's war raged across Florida from coast to coast.

chapter 5

Yo-he-e-hee!

A few days later, scouts brought news to Osceola. Troops led by General Duncan Clinch had left Fort Drane. They headed southwest toward the Withlacoochee River. Nearby lay several Seminole villages. Clinch planned to destroy them and to find Osceola. He led 200 regulars and 460 Florida volunteers.

Early the next morning Osceola broke camp. He wore a blue army coat. It was a trophy from Francis Dade's massacre. Osceola led 250 warriors. They would fight Clinch wherever they found him.

The army moved only twelve miles on December 28. Wagons bogged down. Soldiers suffered from the heat. Their horses muddied the streams before soldiers could drink from them. The column also made a fearful racket. Soldiers had brought their pets with them, so yapping dogs added to the din.

A Canoe

Osceola set his trap. He picked a spot for an ambush. Warriors placed an old canoe for bait.

Scouts could hear them half a mile away. On the third night the army camped three miles from the river.

Osceola set a trap. He picked a spot for an ambush. Warriors placed an old canoe there as bait. They watched to see if Clinch's army used it. At that point the river was 150 feet wide. It ran deep and black. On December 31, the regulars began to cross in the canoe. Two paddlers ferried five men per trip. On the far side of the river was a U-shaped open space. Once across, the regulars rested in this field. They stacked their arms and waited for orders.

It was about noon. Osceola's men moved through the brush, lining the field on three sides. They had trapped the soldiers with the river at their back. One soldier saw something move in the brush. He shouted "Indians! Indians!" Osceola gave the signal to open fire. His shrill war cry carried across the field, "Yo-he-e-hee!"[1] The Seminoles screamed in reply. They fired as the soldiers dived to retrieve their muskets.

The army built forts throughout Florida. When the troops marched between the forts, Seminole attacks killed many soldiers.

After they fired, the warriors dropped flat, rolling to their left to reload. Soldiers aimed where they saw a muzzle flash. Now they would hit nothing.

Soon smoke covered the field. Colonel Alexander Fanning rallied his regulars. When the Seminoles attacked the flanks, he beat them back. The soldiers fixed bayonets. Three times they surged forward. Sixty volunteers crossed the river. They guarded each flank. The soldiers fell back toward the river. First the regulars recrossed the river. Then the volunteers followed. Osceola allowed the army to retreat in peace. It retreated to Fort Drane.

The battle had lasted an hour and a quarter. A third of the regulars suffered wounds. Amazingly only four were killed. Seminole losses were three killed and four wounded. One of the wounded was Osceola. He suffered a wound in his arm.

The enlistments of the volunteers were up. They went home within a week. The few regulars at Fort Drane could not attack again. Osceola sent Clinch a message: "You have guns. So do we. You have powder and lead. So do we. You have men. So do we. Your men will fight. So will ours, until the last drop of Seminoles' blood has moistened the dust of his hunting ground."[2]

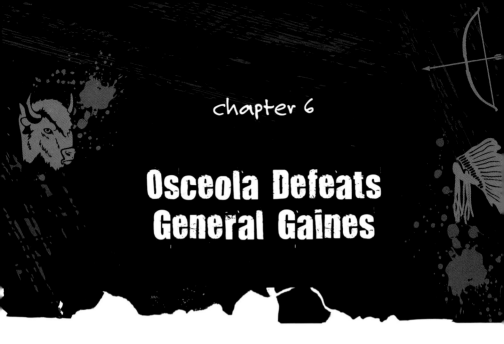

chapter 6

Osceola Defeats General Gaines

O sceola rested for several weeks. His wound was slow to heal. Clearly the fighting would not end quickly. Osceola believed that he could hold out for five years. He knew the land, and his people were united. The warriors obeyed him. The losses were light.[1] Fevers, insects, snakes, and the heat were his allies. Many white soldiers fell ill from malaria and pneumonia. Osceola hoped the U.S. government would tire of fighting in the swamps.

Many whites admired Osceola. One soldier wrote to his father that unfair dealing by the government had caused the war. He thought it might last seven years.[2] Another soldier wrote: "In Osceola . . . was combined a nerve, activity, and intelligence which seemed to diffuse itself among all classes."[3] A newspaper reported, "He is . . . a man of great tact, energy of character, and bold daring."[4]

Army units crossed the state. They searched for Seminole towns that lay deep within the swamplands.

Major General Edward Gaines replaced Duncan Clinch. Gaines arrived in Florida with a thousand soldiers. In mid-February, Gaines's troops left Fort Brooke. He thought they would find a large supply of rations at Fort King. On the way his force found the grim remains of Dade's Massacre. The soldiers buried what remained of the dead. The troops finally reached Fort King. There they found the rations had never been sent! The troops had to head back to Fort Brooke or starve. Gaines's route took him to the Withlacoochee. He hoped to avenge Clinch's defeat there.

Osceola's scouts watched the troops all the way. The soldiers reached the ford on the Withlacoochee River on February 27. More than a thousand Seminoles waited for them on the south bank. The Seminoles opened fire. Quickly the troops felled trees to build a breastwork. The battle became a siege. The troops sent word to Clinch at Fort Drane. If he came quickly he could swing behind the Seminoles, trapping Osceola's men.

Clinch's superior, General Winfield Scott, was angry with Gaines. Scott wanted to defeat Osceola himself. He felt Gaines was robbing him of that honor. So Scott ordered Clinch not to send supplies to Gaines. But the orders said nothing about sending troops. Thus Clinch decided to go to aid Gaines.

The siege entered its eighth day. Gaines had forty-six wounded and five dead. A stray shot hit Gaines in the mouth, causing him to lose one tooth. On March 5, one of

Osceola's men acted on his own. A black, John Caesar, asked the soldiers to talk. The next day Osceola agreed to a truce. Under a white flag he met with soldiers. Osceola's terms were simple. He wanted a promise that the Seminoles could live on their lands in peace. Gaines said he did not have the power to make the promise. He said Osceola must stop the fighting. Only then would Gaines take his request to the government. At that point a distant gunfire broke the truce. It was a signal that Clinch's force had arrived. Osceola and his men dashed from the barricade. They thought Clinch's arrival at that time was a planned trick. The Seminoles faded back into the forest.

The soldiers marched back to Fort Drane. Most were in pitiful shape. They looked like walking skeletons.[5] In March, Gaines left Fort Drane to take up other duties. Once again the Seminoles had defeated U.S. Army troops.

chapter 7

Two New Foes

E arly in 1836, Winfield Scott took the field against Osceola. Scott was a hero of the War of 1812. Now Scott had his orders: He was to defeat the Seminoles once and for all. Scott could have as many troops, supplies, and weapons as he wished.

In March, Scott launched his plan. He divided his force into three groups. The 2,000 men of the right wing would invade Osceola's heartland. They would drive the Seminoles southward. There two forces would await them. The 1,250 men of the center wing would head north from Fort Brooke. They would march to a point near the Withlacoochee. The left wing had the toughest job. Its 1,400 men were to march from the east coast. They would head for a spot near the Dade massacre site. Their route would lead them across some of the roughest terrain in the state.

Osceola was a brilliant leader who made no mistakes.

Osceola was a brilliant leader who made no mistakes. The women and children were well-fed and safe. He kept a good supply of powder and lead. Few Seminoles had lost their lives. Osceola would not bunch his forces. Instead he divided his men into bands of two-hundred warriors. He told them what to do when they met soldiers. If they outnumbered the soldiers, attack. Otherwise let the soldiers pass by.

Scott began the right wing's advance on March 25. For a week the troops slogged through the swamps. The Seminoles flitted ahead from island to island. Scott gave up; there was no way he could catch Osceola. After two weeks the right wing marched to Fort Brooke. The center wing had arrived the day before. It too had no success. The left wing marched from St. Augustine to Fort Brooke. The Seminoles harassed them all the way.

Scott's plan was a failure. It might have worked elsewhere. But it was not suited to fighting Seminoles in the swamps. The army was no closer to defeating Osceola. In April, Scott left Florida. He went to Alabama to fight the Creeks.

General Richard Call then took over the fight. His plan was simple. He would force Osceola into a big battle. If Osceola lost just once, Call thought, his people would desert him. Call waited all summer for more troops. Meanwhile the army had abandoned Fort Drane. So Osceola and his men moved in.

Call's advance reached Fort Drane on October 1. Osceola did not stand and fight as Call wanted. Instead the general found the fort empty. Call pushed on into the Wahoo Swamp. He used

Fort Brooke was located near Tampa Bay.

bloodhounds to track the Seminoles. But the warriors lay in wait. Then they killed the dogs with heavy charges of buckshot.

Call now led two-thousand men. In mid-November they reached the heart of Osceola's stronghold. In the middle of a swamp Call's troops came to a halt. Seminoles fired at them from across a ten-foot stream. The black water looked deep. Call had to decide. Should he use his strength to force a crossing? His men were tired and hungry. It would soon be dark. Call decided to pull back. He retreated fifty miles in five days. In anger President Andrew Jackson relieved Call of his command.

Osceola had defeated another American general. But it was a close call. The stream was only three feet deep. And just beyond it was Osceola's main village. More than six hundred families lived there. Osceola would have had to defend it. Call could have had the big battle he wanted.

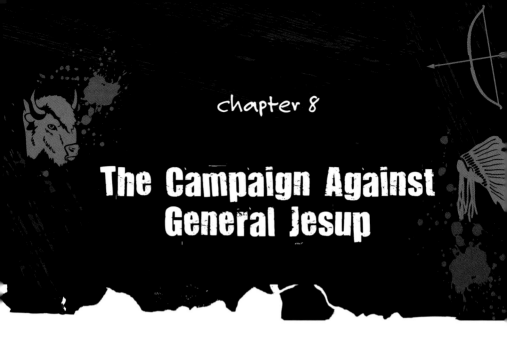

chapter 8

The Campaign Against General Jesup

A new general now led the army. Thomas Jesup hoped to win where others had failed. He was a plodder. He would give the Seminoles no rest. The war had already lasted more than a year. Osceola was worried. His warriors had fought well. But would they fight for another year? He still hoped the whites would tire of the war. Then they would talk of peace. He expected another attack on his stronghold. His bands spread out and moved south.

In March 1837, several chiefs came to Fort Dade. They represented Micanopy. The top chief of the Seminoles had tired of the war. He agreed to give up. The Seminoles would move to the West. The army said they could take their slaves with them. The Seminoles began to assemble at Tampa Bay. The army did not treat them well. It provided them with leaky tents and poor food. The Seminoles also got into fights with the army's Creek allies.

On May 3, Osceola came to Fort Mellon. He said he too would move west. For a few weeks he camped outside the fort. Late in May, Osceola left with two-hundred warriors. He went to Tampa Bay. At midnight he awoke the Seminoles camped there. About seven-hundred joined him and fled north. They were going home.

The escape put Jesup in a bad light. He offered to resign. But the army did not accept his offer.

Hidden food awaited the homecoming of the Seminoles. Crops were ready to harvest. The soldiers did not want to fight in the summer heat. The Seminoles split into small bands. They scattered over central Florida. For the next few months the army was inactive. Jesup planned to resume action in the fall.

The Seminoles suffered that summer. Many tribe members had caught measles from the whites. Others were ill with typhus, yellow fever, and malaria. Osceola himself was not well. A high fever weakened him, and infection pained his wounded arm.[1]

In mid-October, Osceola sent word to Jesup. He would come to St. Augustine to talk about peace. He hoped to work out a compromise.[2] Osceola camped a mile from Fort Payton. General Jesup sent Joseph Hernandez to talk with him. Hernandez was to decide whether the talks were productive. If not, Jesup ordered him to seize all of Osceola's party.

A flag of truce flew over Osceola's camp. In fact, the whites had provided the white cloth for him to use. Mounted

Osceola was taken prisoner without a shot.

troops numbering 250 circled the camp. Hernandez came forward to talk. Osceola said he was not ready to surrender. However Osceola did want to make peace. As proof he offered to turn in some runaway slaves. In reply Hernandez gave a signal. The dragoons closed in. Then, as Jesup had ordered, they took the Seminoles prisoners. The breach of trust stunned the Seminoles. They did not fire a shot.

A witness said Osceola did not look surprised. It was just one more betrayal by whites.[3] The soldiers placed Osceola, who looked ill, in chains. Then they put him on a horse to take him to Fort Marion, north of St. Augustine. The soldiers took eighty-two other prisoners.

Word began to spread that Osceola's capture took place under a white flag. Newspaper accounts attacked Jesup. They said his act of treachery would prolong the war. No other Seminoles would be willing to talk peace. Jesup would spend the rest of his life trying to explain his action.

chapter 9

Death in Captivity

Thomas Jesup put Osceola in prison at Fort Marion. The Spanish had begun building the coastal fort in 1672. Its six-foot-thick limestone walls prevented escapes. Osceola's cell was a stone vault. Straw covered the floor, and forage bags served as bedding. Osceola was very ill, suffering from chills, aches, and fevers. Osceola's two wives and two children joined him in prison. In late November some of the Seminoles broke out of Fort Marion. Osceola was too weak to go with them. The escape angered Jesup. To prevent other escapes, he sent Osceola to Fort Moultrie. It lay on an island in Charleston Harbor, South Carolina. Osceola had his own room. He was allowed to move about the fort at will.

Even as a prisoner, Osceola was famous. The skilled artist George Catlin came to Fort Moultrie. By day Catlin painted Osceola's portrait. At night the two talked about the war. The people of Charleston flocked to the fort to see Osceola.

An iron fence protects Osceola's grave at Fort Moultrie, South Carolina.

This lithograph, published after the war ended, shows bloodhounds physically assaulting the Seminoles. The army used bloodhounds to track the Seminoles after other attempts at tracking failed. It was the Florida territorial government that purchased a pack of bloodhounds in early 1840. After a public outcry against this practice, the Secretary of War issued an order that dogs be kept muzzled and leashed while being used for tracking. Since bloodhounds cannot track through water, the Seminoles easily evaded them.

He talked with some of them. Osceola knew English but would not speak it. He always used an interpreter.

Osceola's fever worsened. Doctor Frederick Weedon tried a treatment of the time. He drained some of Osceola's blood. He believed this would draw out the illness. But the treatment only further weakened Osceola.

On January 30, Osceola's tonsils swelled. He could no longer talk. Osceola dressed himself for the last time. Slowly he donned shirt, leggings, and moccasins. He slid his war knife into its sheath. With red powder he smeared his face, neck, and hands. He then placed his turban with three plumes on his head. His wives eased him down onto a pillow. In a last effort he drew his knife. He placed it on his chest and died. He was only thirty-three.

Dr. Weedon cut off Osceola's head and embalmed it. In 1843, he sent it to a museum in New York City. It was lost in a fire in 1866. The rest of Osceola's body was buried near the fort. The grave marker reads:

OSCEOLA

Patriot and Warrior

Died at Fort Moultrie

January 30th, 1838

The war did not end with Osceola's capture. The Seminoles fought on. General Zachary Taylor pursued them for two years. And General Walker Armistead followed him in 1840. From time to time small bands gave up. By March 1842, it was thought that only 300 Seminoles remained in Florida. The U.S. government had shipped more than 3,800 to the West.

In the West, the Seminoles lived among the Creeks. In 1869, they received their own land. Over the years land grabbers stole most of it. Little of this land remains today. In Florida few whites saw the Seminoles. The 1900 census guessed their number at four hundred. They lived in the Everglades in open-sided thatched homes called *chickees*. Dugout canoes carried them through the swamps.

Florida set up four reservations. Today about two-thousand Seminoles live on them.[1] The tribe has never signed a peace treaty with the United States. Still the Seminoles are U.S. citizens. Some make items to sell to tourists. Others work for owners of nearby farms. By surviving they won the war that Osceola began.

Glossary

allies—People who have promised to fight alongside one another.

band—A subdivision of a tribe, sometimes only a few dozen in number.

chief—A leader of a band or tribe; often a chief was limited to a specific role, such as leadership in war.

council—A meeting of the adults in a tribe; all warriors had the right to express their opinions.

Creeks—A tribe formerly living in the southeastern United States.

forage bags—Heavy canvas sacks used for carrying food and grain.

ford—A shallow stretch of a stream, suitable for crossing by men and horses.

medicine man—A Native American priest who practiced medicine, foretold the future, and gave advice.

rations—An allotment of food, often equal to one person's daily needs.

reservation—An area set aside by the government to be the permanent home of a group of Native Americans.

scouts—Skilled frontiersmen; scouts served as lookouts, read tracks, found trails, and located game.

treaties—Agreements between two governments; treaties between Native Americans and whites often dealt with sale of land.

tribe—A large group of Native Americans who speak a common language and live in the same area.

truce—An agreement to suspend fighting.

warrior—An adult Native American fighting man.

Chapter Notes

Author's Note

1. Marion E. Gridley, *The Story of the Seminole* (New York: G. P. Putnam's Sons, 1973), p. 51.

Chapter 1

1. M. M. Cohen, *Notices of Florida and the Campaigns* (Charleston, Burges & Honour, S.C.: 1836), p. 62.

2. Ibid., p. 273.

3. John Sprague, *The Florida War* (New York: Appleton and Co., 1848), p. 86.

4. William and Ellen Hartley, *Osceola: The Unconquered Indian* (New York: Hawthorn Books, 1973), p. 130.

5. Woodbourne Potter, *The War in Florida* (Baltimore Lewis & Coleman,: 1836), pp. 96–97.

Chapter 2

1. William and Ellen Hartley, *Osceola: The Unconquered Indian*, p. 58.

Chapter 3

1. *Fletcher v. Peck*, 6 Cranch 87.

Chapter 5

1. William and Ellen Hartley, *Osceola: The Unconquered Indian*, p. 155.
2. Charles Coe, *Red Patriots* (The Editor Pub. Co., Cincinnati : 1898), p. 65.

Chapter 6

1. Hartley, p. 159.
2. Edwin McReynolds, *The Seminoles* (Norman, Okla.: University of Oklahoma, 1957), p. 157.
3. Sprague, p. 161.
4. St. Augustine *Herald*, January 13, 1836.
5. John Bemrose, *Reminiscences of the Second Seminole War* (Tallahassee: University of Florida, 1966), cited by Clifford Lindsey Alderman, Osceola and the Seminole Wars (New York: Julian Messner,1973), p. 108.

Chapter 8

1. Ben Stahl, *Osceola, Seminole Leader* (New York: William Morrow, 1976), p. 81.
2. May McNeer, *War Chief of the Seminoles* (New York: Random House, 1954), p. 108.
3. Clifford Lindsey Alderman, *Osceola and the Seminole Wars* (New York: Julian Messner,1973), p. 161.

Chapter 9

1. Merwyn Garbarino, *The Seminoles* (New York: Chelsea House, 1989), p. 105.

Further Reading

Books

Bland, Celia. *Osceola: Seminole Rebel*. New York: Chelsea House, 1994.

Gibson, Karen Bush. *Native American History for Kids*. Chicago, Ill: Chicago Review Press, 2010.

Koestler-Grack, Rachel A. *Osceola, 1804-1838*. Mankato, Minn.: Blue Earth Books, 2003.

Sayre, Gordon M. *The Indian Chief as Tragic Hero: Native Resistance and the Literatures of America, From Moctezuma to Tecumseh*. North Carolina: University of North Carolina Press, 2005.

Sneve, Virginia Driving Hawk. *The Seminoles*. New York: Holiday House, 1994.

Viola, Herman J. Viola. *Osceola*. Austin, Tex.: Raintree Steck-Vaughn, 1993.

Internet Addresses

Myths and Dreams: Exploring the Cultural Legacies of Florida and the Caribbean—Seminole Chief Osceola

<http://www.kislakfoundation.org/millennium-exhibit/profiles6.htm>

Seminole Tribe of Florida—History: Osceola and Abiaka

<http://www.semtribe.com/History/OsceolaandAbiaka.aspx>

Index